Insect World

Termites

by Mari Schuh

Bullfrog
Books

Ideas for Parents and Teachers

Bullfrog Books let children practice reading informational text at the earliest reading levels. Repetition, familiar words, and photo labels support early readers.

Before Reading

- Discuss the cover photo. What does it tell them?
- Look at the picture glossary together. Read and discuss the words.

Read the Book

- "Walk" through the book and look at the photos. Let the child ask questions. Point out the photo labels.
- Read the book to the child, or have him or her read independently.

After Reading

- Prompt the child to think more. Ask: How are termites like other insects? Can you think of other insects that build nests?

Bullfrog Books are published by Jump!
5357 Penn Avenue South
Minneapolis, MN 55419
www.jumplibrary.com

Copyright © 2015 Jump! International copyright reserved in all countries. No part of this book may be reproduced in any form without written permission from the publisher.

Library of Congress Cataloging-in-Publication Data

Schuh, Mari C., 1975-
  Termites / by Mari Schuh.
    pages cm. -- (Insect world)
  Summary: "This photo-illustrated book for early readers tells how termites live in colonies, make nests, and find food. Includes picture glossary"-- Provided by publisher.
  Audience: 5-8.
  Audience: Grade K to 3.
  Includes bibliographical references and index.
  ISBN 978-1-62031-087-8 (hardcover) --
ISBN 978-1-62496-155-7 (ebook)
  1. Termites--Juvenile literature. I. Title.
II. Series: Schuh, Mari C., 1975- Insect world.
  QL529.S37 2015
  595.7'36--dc23
                                    2013042381

Series Editor: Rebecca Glaser
Series Designer: Ellen Huber
Book Designer: Anna Peterson
Photo Researcher: Kurtis Kinneman

All photos by Shutterstock except: Alex Wild, 6–7, 8 (inset), 11, 23ml, 23tl; GEORGE GRALL/National Geographic Creative, 14; Konmesa|Dreamstime.com, 16–17; Minden Pictures/SuperStock, 8–9, 20–21; Minden, 22

Printed in the United States of America at Corporate Graphics, in North Mankato, Minnesota.
6-2014
10 9 8 7 6 5 4 3 2 1

Dedicated to Brantley Quam—MS

Table of Contents

Busy Termites

Look! A nest!

See the bugs?
They are termites.

Termites live in a colony.

Each one has a job.

Soldier termites are guards.

Oh, no! Army ants!

They fight.

Go away ants!

army
ant

See the queen?

She has a job, too.

She lays eggs.

queen

eggs

She can lay 30,000 eggs in a day.

worker termite

Worker termites
eat wood.

Munch. Munch.

It's their job.

They spit it up.

They feed it
to the colony.

The workers make nests.
Dig. Dig.

14

wood

They tunnel in wood.

Some nests are made
in soil.

See the nest?

It is damp.

It is dark.

nest

Wow! A tall nest!

It is a mound.

It's made of dirt and spit.

It's made of poop, too!

Termites work hard.

The nest is big.

Good job, bugs!

Parts of a Termite

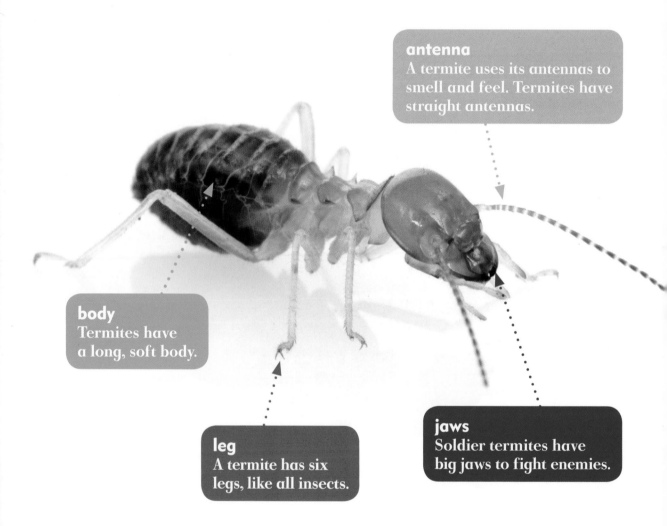

antenna
A termite uses its antennas to smell and feel. Termites have straight antennas.

body
Termites have a long, soft body.

leg
A termite has six legs, like all insects.

jaws
Soldier termites have big jaws to fight enemies.

Picture Glossary

army ant
A kind of ant that hunts for food in big groups.

queen
A female termite that lays eggs.

colony
A group of termites that live together.

soldier termite
A termite that keeps the nest safe from enemies.

nest
A home where termites live and raise young termites.

worker termite
A termite that makes the nest, searches for food, and feeds the colony.

Index

To Learn More

Learning more is as easy as 1, 2, 3.

1) Go to www.factsurfer.com

2) Enter "termites" into the search box.

3) Click the "Surf" button to see a list of websites.

With factsurfer.com, finding more information is just a click away.